A M O R

F A T I

Disclaimer

The views and opinions expressed in this book are solely those of the author, Jadan Washington, and do not necessarily reflect the official policy or position of any agency of the author's past or present employers. The content of Amor Fati: Poems Curated by Fate has been provided for informational and entertainment purposes only.

Every effort has been made to ensure that the content of this book is accurate and beneficial to the reader. However, due to the nature of personal interpretation of art and literature, the author assumes no responsibility for any personal interpretations or reactions to the content. The author and publisher are not liable for any misunderstandings, incidents, or damages resulting from the interpretation and application of the information contained within this book.

Readers are encouraged to reflect upon the poems and their themes with an open mind and heart, understanding that poetry is a deeply personal and subjective form of expression that resonates differently with each individual.

ISBN: 979-8-9904259-0-3 (paperback)
ISBN: 979-8-9904259-1-0 (ebook)
Book design by Nuno Moreira, NM DESIGN

AMOR
FATI

poems curated
by fate

JADAN
WASHINGTON

TABLE OF CONTENTS

TABLE OF CONTENTS

WELCOME

My poetry represents my soul
If you dare to explore, you can understand my true story,
my hidden secrets
But prepare to feel hurt
Prepare to scream
Prepare for a fight because my inner writer is a cynic
There is no happiness here but I'm trying

WHO I WANT

I will fall in love with an artist in the future
He will create beautiful things and others will recognize
his glory
They'll respect his thoughts and value them as if they
carry the weight of the world
He'll shine and this never-ending glow will chase away
the darkness of others
He'll be happy
He is me and I cannot wait to fall in love with the person
I hope to become

AM I BACK?

For the first time in years, words flow free
I've kept them locked in a golden cage
Deep in the shadows of my mind where nothing else existed
No surprise, the words are back
I guess it's true that nothing last forever

UNKNOWING

I feel bare around you
Completely open and available for you to tear apart
I'm used to pretending to be strong
But with you—I am weak
With you, I feel powerful
But with you, I am powerless
With you, I feel hopeful
But with you, I am insecure
With you, I feel untouchable
But most importantly, with you, I think I've found myself

DREAM ENGRAVED HEART

Tonight, I dreamt of you
I wish I could save the images and store them away
I would engrave them in my brain or trap them in a
locket, wrapped around my heart
We know that's impossible so I'm writing this before the
images fade away
Hold on, I'm losing focus...

What happened again?

Oh yes, in my dream you and I were alone sharing
thoughts and ironically, dreams
I shared with you visions of future-us and your face lit up
I'm closing my eyes now and still can see that look on
your face
One full of admiration and promise
Maybe one day I'll see the look in person
Until then, I'll just keep the dream engraved on my heart

THE CALL

Fate, stay the night so I can dream again
Destiny, hear my call, I'm shouting at the wind
Kismet, bless my soul so I can feel again

IT'S NOT OVER

Lonely boy, I see you wandering in the night
You always have a faraway look on your face but I can
read your thoughts
I see you're trying to convince yourself to live
Beautiful boy, come take a look
I'll show you a world that only we can see
We'll perform a duet written by nature
Soulmate, soulmate
Are you ready for the stars to be our spotlight?

THE PEOPLE'S PRINCE

I want you
Not lustfully but spiritually and emotionally
I feel as if our souls will light up the sky and create new
colors of life
We'd connect on a level that I've never felt before
I'd share my art and you'd match it with your quick wit
and sounds of joy
Are you my muse?
Or, am I yours?

FIND ME

I'm ready to fall into the sky and land in clouds of love
Wrap me in support and warm words of reassurance
Make me cry tears of joy as my heart beats faster and my
soul sings
Then watch me rip it from my chest so it can connect
with yours
My body is vibrating with the anticipation of you
I hope our souls like each other
They will mingle and mix until we are a new entity of
devotion and strength
I wish to close my eyes and forever feel your presence in
my mind and your lips on my body
I'm sending signals to the universe so you can find me
Are you close?

HERE I AM

Here I am again, a lost lover boy pining after something
that never was
Here I am again, musing over someone who never
thought about me once
Here I am again, wondering was this connection imaginary?
Here I am again, asking why I'm not enough
Here I am again, thinking maybe I'm just dramatic
Here I am again, hoping that he will wake up and realize
I'm still here
Here I am again, wishing on a dead star that can't fulfill this
Here I am again, writing a sad note
Here I am again, afraid to expose the reason that I only
care for those who can't give what I want
Here I am again, wondering *why I'm so broken?*
And here I am again, asking *why am I still fighting for him?*

FROZEN

Cold of heart, they call me
I breathe ice onto the field of my interactions and let the
frost trickle over each word
But how is it possible that my iced soul is less damaging
than yours, that radiates light?
You're full of promise and emotion yet you're so naive
I'm heartless but have managed to not cause as much
pain as you
How does it feel to know that the cold one understands more?
The man who freezes hearts is warmer than you

NO FEAR

There's so much sound in the night
But why are people so afraid?
If you ask, someone will tell a story about monsters you
cannot see
But really, it's because the shadows hold the most secrets
The moon controls the tides of emotion you have tried to
hold back with blue skies and clouds of lies
There is no silence in the night
Shadows are filled with rustling of trees and sobs of the
honest
I embrace the time when Sister Moon is released from her
prison
I love it because we both are free
I've made friends with the unknown
Monsters and all the rustling trees
The shadows wrap around me and supply comfort while I
pour out
I've made friends with Sister Moon and I suggest you do too

WHAT DOES IT MEAN?

Inhibition

A feeling that makes one self-conscious

Self-consciousness

Unsure awareness of oneself

Self-awareness is key but not when it holds you back

Not when it causes you to question your own thoughts
and worth

Countless times I've asked myself, "is this worth it?"

Shall I continue on this journey waiting for an untimely end?

I still don't know the answer

Logic

Reasoning conducted or assessed according to strict
principles of validity

A logical answer is that my life is worth something so the
only answer is to keep fighting

Unfortunately, there's still a piece that causes me to doubt this

To doubt myself

Confusion

THE ENEMY

Each word I speak of the future is a string of blasphemy
Every consonant feels like stabbing needles
When I talk to others about what our lives might be like, I
cry on the inside
Chats of goals and love to come, shakes me to the core
I can believe the hype for a second but then IT slams into me
IT stabs at me in the chest and tells my heart it won't feel
the glow of happiness
Little soldiers of despair travel through each limb, causing
me to lock up and feel as heavy as my invisible tears
IT can cause the air to disappear from my lungs
Missing breath dangles out of reach
I scream for help but there is no one that can fix this
The strings of fate have already been twisted and mine
are just about to be cut
Shadows set by just one look at IT
One look into IT'S eyes
One glance into the face of reality

INTERMISSION

I NEED A BREAK. SEE YOU IN A SECOND

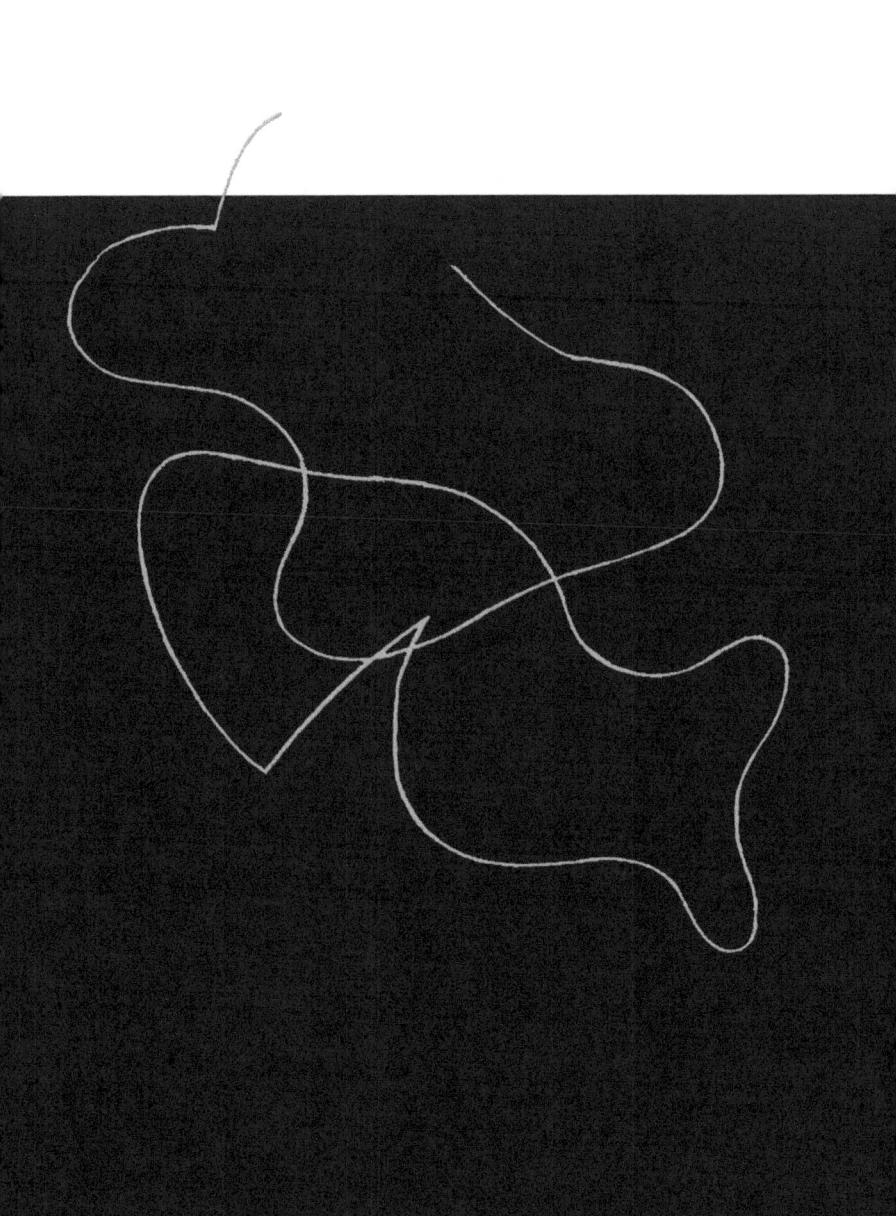

HE'S BACK

My creativity died in the winter but it's back with the heat
of summer
Now at night, I sit under my twinkling friends and write
my deepest secrets and dramatic woes
Art is odd; I sat down thinking that my ability was gone
but here I am, writing this beautiful song
I've kept my emotions buried underneath frost but
fortunately, that first ray of sunshine appeared
I hope you're ready because I think I am

TAKE IT AWAY

The night sky is a beautiful reflection of my feelings
Endless and empty one moment but ablaze with life in
another

YOU

I welcome emptiness

I wish my heart did not beat and my blood did not sing

for every possible emotion and conquest

How great it could be if my tears didn't appear in the darkest

of night, when doors are locked and old memories swirl

I don't miss anyone or anything but I do miss myself in

past memories

I miss the person who was more happier than not

The boy who felt he still had a chance to be enveloped in

joy and love

CRUSHES

I've found that crushes are accurately named
What am I being crushed by though?
Fear? Maybe a little
Anxiety? Not yet
Hope? Yes, that's it
I discovered hope to be the scariest of them all

I can overcome fear and anxiety as easily as I've learned
to tie my shoes but why run away from hope and promise?
You need hope to get up in the morning
"I hope today will be a good day" you say
Tonight, you will recite your shitty day but tomorrow you
hope for a better one
The thought of hope can turn on you very quickly
As hope crushes down on me, I've decided I won't hope
we get together or fall in love
I'm hoping I find peace with whatever happens to us

RUN BEFORE IT'S TOO LATE

Riding the moonlight's wave, hoping to catch my fate
I see the end right there but I don't think I'll win this race
Something about our connection scares me
I've been here before and I fear this time will be worse
I can look into your eyes and see my broken heart staring
back at me

THE OFFER

I'll trade you the ocean for just a touch
I'll offer the grass for your trust
And I might give up the stars for your love

INSANITY

I keep telling myself that you are mine
I'm going to break when I found out the truth
The truth of delusion and sanity
I think our hearts are intertwined, riding the same rhythm
My heart is repeatedly beating but yours is syncopated
and irregular
We aren't meant for each other and I know we never will be

EMBARRASSMENT

His whole life he wanted to visit the moon
Research was performed for hours and an expensive
telescope was purchased
He'd sit under the sky, talking about unknown details
As the sun rose, he'd pray for a chance to fly and visit
what he thought was home
His friend challenged him to pursue this obsession but the
boy always said, "It's impossible"
One night, time froze before the sun could appear, the sky
spoke
"We have a shared friend that loves you", the stars
chorused
Their friend had been offered a chance to wish on the
brightest star which would allow anything to come true
As the boy sat, listening to the twinkling shapes, his
irritation grew, "Get on with the point"
The stars were shocked
Is this the boy their friend raved about?
Oh well. It wasn't their business
The stars let the boy know that their friend decided to
pass and offer him the wish instead
He froze for a moment but melted quickly

The stars expected a longer pause but his response came
fast, "Not interested"
The dream of reaching the moon was just that— a dream
It was not a reality he would work for
He never worked for anything really
Stars were shocked but they allowed time to resume and
the Sun rose
As they disappeared and clustered together, gossip grew
Some were confused, shattered, but they all found it
humorous
They knew their friend struggled with his own demons
After a secret discussion with Fate, the stars learned his
journey had a war on the horizon
This broken child had wasted his reprieve on someone
with no ambition...something he swore to never do
In between their giggles, the stars decided to make their
own wish
They hoped their friend learned that love is never meant
to be a sacrifice of oneself

SUPERMAN

I know I'm stronger than you and will be forever
100 pounds sat on my chest but I chose to battle the
25-pound baggage you won't fight
More weight, more strife, more despair
                              But I must help you
I had to make sure you'll be okay
We both are sinking ships but at every chance, I brought
myself lower to provide support and offer you more air

BRIGHT

I cried while staring at the sunset
It was so beautiful that it hurt
I'm trying to imagine what it feels like to be stared at and
have your beauty revered
I feel like a failure and a waste of space
I want to be a sunset

UNDERSTANDING

I've learned that feeling worthless is easier than knowing
you deserve the world
When you understand that mountains should shift and
diamonds deserve to be gifted, the fallacies feel worse
If you understand your worth, it's harder when friends
stop calling
You cry harder when the lies spread faster

INTERMISSION #2

My biggest skill is knowing when to walk away
So, take a beat, little mouse, and realize you're going too fast
It's happening right now
My brain is weak and nothing feels real
Time for another break

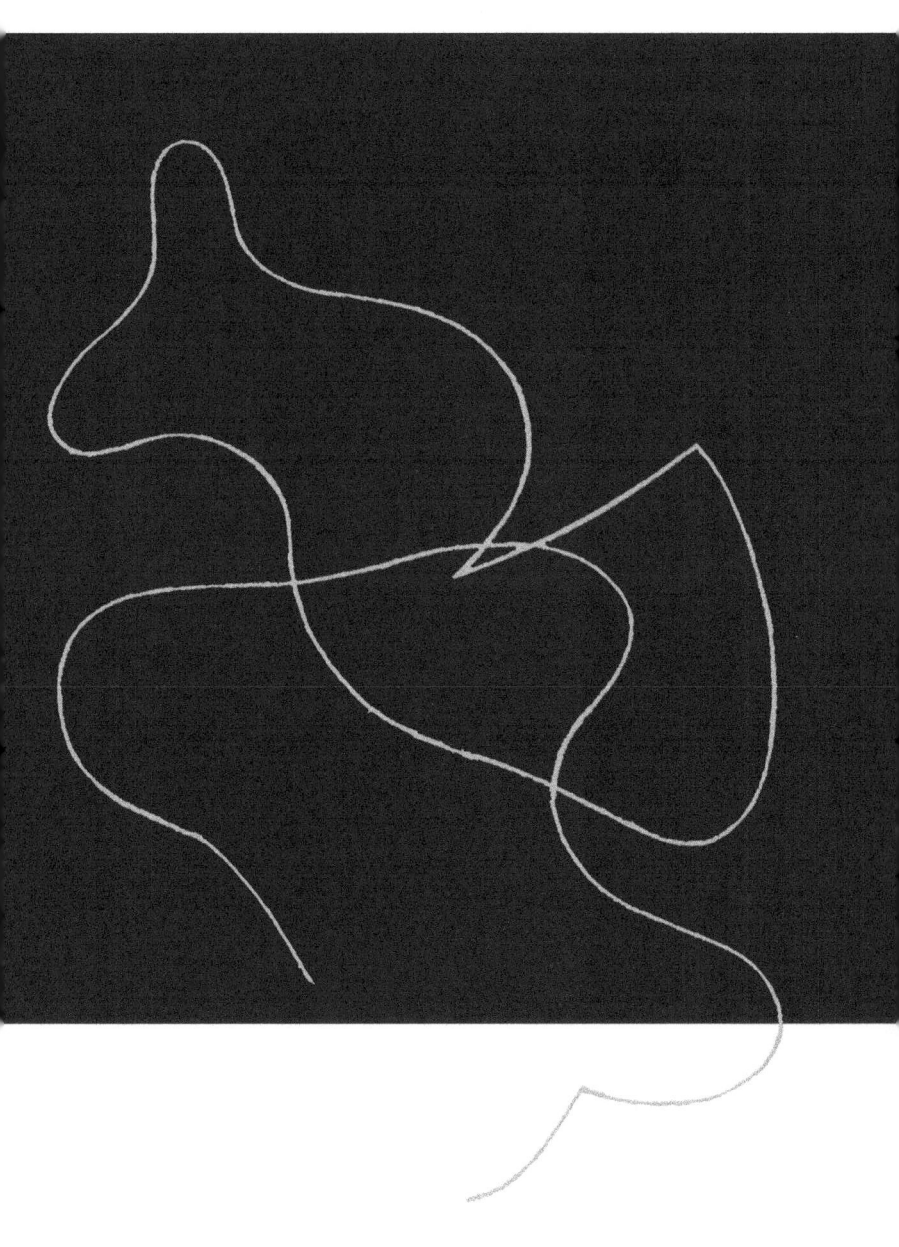

NO DIAGNOSES

The only time this physical pain stops is when I close
my eyes, push it to the back of my mind, and focus on
imaginary outcomes
With my eyes forced shut, I know there is a long life ahead
I can stupidly predict that my dreams are around the
corner just like a lost love could be
But remember, I know this isn't reality

I should open my eyes but I'm afraid
I fear what I have to face
Reality has stripped me of true passion and progress
I'm stuck
Should I keep performing this lie or embrace reality?
Shall I pretend that things will change or slap myself into
oblivion?

HONESTY

During a time when I should feel like a priority…
I somehow know loneliness the most
During a time where love should be strong and shine like
a diamond…
I am a toy for the creatures of the darkness
During a time where I should believe in the support of
many…
I question the word of the few
They say actions speak louder than words but what do
you do when everyone is frozen AND mute?

THE TRUTH #1

Sometimes I think the stars are just our dazzling hopes
staring back at us
As we wish harder, more will shine
but recently I've started to think they're just tools to taunt us

INCOMING OF SPITE

Fire engulfs my heart and future

My emotions have slowly been incinerated until I'm left
on this path

The path of a hardened shell

A shell of a person who stares at death like an upcoming
appointment

Has my soul retreated into a far corner, waiting for a blast
of light to illuminate purpose?

Or maybe it's gone forever

Will I always be this jaded person affected by the
combination of past and present?

Or will I find my resurrection?

Hmmm I don't know but both sounds so tempting

RECOMMENDATION: SLEEP

Lately dreams have plagued me

Dreams I wish to ignore

Dreams I want to unsee

In my sleep, I see visions of support and strength

I'm happy and glowing

Unbothered

So, what's my problem?

Why shouldn't I want to see this beautiful sight?

Feel the vibrations of those speaking words of love

My issue is that I wake up

No matter how tight I hold on, the dreams do not manifest

TREATMENT PLAN: SLEEP

When reality constricts and it feels like the world is
closing in, sleep is usually my only escape
Now, my dreams are no longer a safe space
I close my eyes and dark questions float across the back of
my eyelids
Why must we die all the time?
Why do we cry?
How can I imagine a better future when the past and
present are cycles of death?

THE TRUTH #2

"When you wish upon a star, it makes no difference who you are.
Anything will happen, your heart desires will come to you"

I must be wishing on a dead star or one that knows fate
has already decided my path
Wishing for simple things which have been inverted to
cause pain
Fate has an odd way of making sure everything I've
wanted doesn't come true
So, where does that leave me?
I'm a sad lover boy, glutton for punishment
I know that nothing comes to me
So, why do I keep wishing?
Does this make me hopelessly delusional or just stupid?

DEATH DATE: AUGUST 23RD

My father, My father
You tightly hid your rainbow underneath your skin
So, I know you never expected your only seed to wear his
as armor
My father, My father
While you were afraid of those finding out your biggest
secret, my biggest fear was the idea of lying my entire life
My father, My father
When I stepped out of my cocoon at 14, you weren't
ready to reveal your flag
But you chose to split your skin and let me take a peek
My father, My father
Though you only took a quick, shadowed step out the
closet, I will always respect the difficulty
My father, My father
I miss you

SILENT FILM

Life is a beautiful nightmare
I cry as I live through it but stand with mouth agape as
the scenery passes
It's a night terror full of sweet kisses and broken promises
I want this sad dream to disappear like a selective
memory but I know it shouldn't
It's time to appear in the scene, my lucid dreamer
Wake yourself up and take control
Life is a beautiful nightmare
As my eyes flicker open, the nightmare will end and the
fake love will fade away

THE ATTACK

Today your memory tried to strangle me
I hallucinated your voice
Saw your image stepping up to me
I've made the choice to move into the future
But the forces know this is your last chance to drag me down
There's no fight in me as selective memories pound my body
I felt you
I smelt you
Why am I allowing memories of the past to create trouble
for myself?

LANGUAGE BARRIER

Mon amour
Can you promise to stay?
I'm fighting to lower the walls and allow you in
You'll see what life is like once I take off the mask and
stop performing
But only if you promise to wait for me

Mi corazón
I've been perfectly casted as the world's punching bag so,
I don't understand your statement
Why promise to take care of me?
I'm only asking you to stay, don't add on foolish
statements
Don't complicate what needs a simple response

My light
I stand up for myself
Your gestures are kind but unnecessary
I don't want you to become my shield
Just promise me you'll stay

Amor aeternus

I need a vow

Nothing is real until the words are spoken

I don't care that you're offering a carved-out heart

What is an action when I need words

Ex amanté

I realize how I wronged us

I'm used to glittery lies and customized hymns

You offered your version of everything but I couldn't take it

Still, I don't get it

Why couldn't you just promise?

FOLLOW

Little mouse
Scurry from the shadow and throw open your window
Pitch yourself from your tower but make sure to land
It's time to explore the woods
Winter is gone and so are the excuses

THE CONVERSATION

Who are we?

Are we the future?

The muses of masses?

No mistake can be made or this will be a waste

Time is spinning fast so, I'm begging

Be honest

Be open

This journey has many dangers but that's how we know

it's right

We're accepting the pressure because it feels correct

These are the hardest truths that can't be ran from

It must be time to step away from the mirror and speak to

myself later

CLOSURE IS NOT REAL

The possible turning of tides has me thinking of you
Not out of spite or a plot for revenge but to honor the past
You've seen me struggle through life and when I didn't
have a will to live, you shared yours
For so long you were my special rock as I fought the
others that weighed me down

Let me say thank you
Thank you for being part of my perception of living
Thank you for loving me in your special but imperfect way
And thank you for breaking me so I could learn that I can
manage on my own

I have no contact for you — nor do I want one
All I need is the reaction I've constructed in my mind

TRUST

Are you extraordinary if no one tells you so?
Where is the line between confidence and delusion?
Everyone has an opinion but nobody has the answer
I decided I don't care
I'm choosing to stomp through life extraordinarily delusional

TO BE CONTINUED

I heard that Fate and Choice are enemies
Rumors began and no amount of debate has been able to
silence them
Some argue your path is predetermined or a collection of
tiny decisions
In my mind, Fate and Choice are conjoined
Fate absorbs your energy to create a map
Once the map is created you choose where the journey begins
As you encounter the obstacles Fate throws, it's your
choice to fight
Remember, this is the proclamation of an all-star pessimist
I'm going through my journey and have cursed the map I
was handed
In silent moments, I still wonder if this life is a cautionary
tale for others
I'll admit I'm a work in progress

AN EXPLANATION

This book is a timeline of writings and correlating emotions. We go in order, starting with early pieces from 2016 and continuing to 2024. I looked through over 200 poems I finished or tried to finish to create this book. There was a time when I felt writing was the only way of expressing myself since there were only a few who could openly listen and understand.

Often, my writing was a form of self-talk or a process piece, a term I've learned in more recent months. This never felt like a journal entry since too much thought and passion was put into the creation of them. I've stated boldly: I'm an artist. A creative. I would routinely write and if no new material was being created, I'd go back to edit work from years prior.

Originally, I had no intention of releasing these. My biggest reason was because they're so personal. Any creative work or art is, but every written piece of mine explains vulnerable emotions and connects to challenging moments in my life. I can read each piece and explain the inspiration, and situation, and tell you when it was first written. At this stage in my life, I have no interest in doing that though. That's TOO real but I won't say I'll never do it. I'm learning to not cut opportunities out just because of fear.

ABOUT THE AUTHOR

Jadan Washington hails from Connecticut with an affinity for creativity and artistic endeavor. His journey began as an avid lover of theater and music before transitioning into high-fashion and media - yet behind the scenes he was piecing together his story through writing. By facing personal challenges head-on and practicing self-expression and growth strategies through writing, *Amor Fati: Poems Curated by Fate* is his heartfelt exploration of love, hope and healing, interwoven with themes such as destiny and dreams. This collection gives an intimate view into the process of self-discovery!